Appetizer Recipes

Table of Contents

Easy Herb Spread
English Muffin Crab Cakes
Five Cheese Baked Ziti
Fried Meat Ravioli
Fried Mozzarella with Roasted Pepper Sauce
Fried Tomatoes
Garlic and Blue Cheese Bread
Garlic Clam Dip
Sauteed Goat Cheese Cakes
Hot Stuffed Mushrooms
Hot Wings
Italian Bread Boat Dip
Jumbo Garlic Shrimp
Little Franks with Orange Dipping Sauce
Marinated Mushrooms
Mashed Potato Stuffed Mushrooms
Mexican Dip
Mixed Cheese Spread
Mozzarella Sticks with Spicy Sauce
Mushroom and Nut Pate
Mushroom & Sun Dried Tomato Spread
Mushroom Bread
Onion Rings with Dipping Sauce
Pancake Syrup Chicken Wings
Peanut Chili Dip
Pesto Crescents
Pierogies with Sour Cream
Pork Tenderloin with Roasted Garlic Mayonnaise
Quick Stuffed Celery
Raisin Spread
Red Bell Pepper Pancakes
Salmon Dip
Salsa with Shrimp
Sausage Dip
Sauteed Mushrooms
Sauteed Mushrooms in Biscuits

Anchovy Antipasto

1/2 cup vegetable oil
3 anchovy fillets, finely chopped
1 can of tuna, drained and mashed
1 6 oz. jar marinated artichoke hearts, drained and cut up
1 small bag of baby greens
2 tbsp. lemon juice
4 tomatoes cut into 8 slices each
8 slices of pepperoni

Preparation:

1. In small bowl combine anchovy, oil and lemon juice. Let stand.

2. Pour anchovy mixture into larger bowl and add all ingredients except baby greens. Mix well.

3. Place baby greens on individual dishes and pour mixture ontop of greens.

4. Serve.

Apple and Brie Fondue

2 lbs. brie cheese
5 apples, peeled and cut into slices

Preparation:

1. Remove rind from cheese and cut into cubes.

2. Place cheese in fondue dish. Heat until cheese has melted but not liguidy.

3. Serve apple slices to dip into cheese. You can use teared pieces of italian bread also.

Artichoke Dip

1 can artichoke hearts, chopped up
5 scallions, chopped
6 garlic cloves, minced
2 tsp. butter
1 8 oz. whipped cream cheese
2 cups sour cream
1 cup muenster cheese

1. Preheat oven to 350 degrees.

2. Grease small baking dish.

3. In medium bowl combine all ingredients.

4. Place in greased baking dish and bake for 10 minutes.

5. Serve with crackers.

Artichokes and Shrimp Dip

8 whole artichokes
¼ cup olive oil
¼ cup lemon juice
2 tsp. salt
1 tsp. rosemary
2 4½ oz. cans shrimp
3/4 cup mayonnaise
2 tbs.. dijon mustard
2 tsp. tarragon
1 bay leaf
¼ tsp. pepper
1 tsp. Worcestershire sauce
½ cup onion, minced

1. Wash and trim artichokes leaves. Cook artichokes in boiling water. About 1 inch deep. Add to the water lemon juice, salt, pepper, bay leaf, tarragon and rosemary. Cook for about 45 minutes or until leaves pull off easily.

2. To make shrimp sauce you add mayonnaise, mustard, Worcestershire sauce, onions and shrimp. Mix all ingredients well.

3. Place shrimp dip in ramekins and artichokes on one plate each. Makes nice appetizer or first course.

Arugala Salad with Balsamic Vinegar Dressing

3 garlic cloves, chopped
1½ lbs. arugala
1 pint cherry tomatoes, halved
3 tbsp. balsamic vinegar
½ cup olive oil
2 shallots, minced
¼ tsp. salt

1. In small bowl or blender mix together garlic, balsamic vinegar, olive oil, shallots and salt.

2. In large bowl add in arugala and tomatoes. Pour over dressing and serve.

Asparagus Cream Cheese Spread

1 16 oz. whipped cream cheese
2 cans asparagus
4 scallions, chopped
3 tbsp. horseradish sauce
6 slices bacon
pinch salt

1. Cook bacon in microwave or fry. Let cool and break up into tiny small pieces.

2. Place all ingredients into food processor or blender. Mix well.

3. Refrigerate for 1 hour before serving.

4. Serve with vegetables, breads or crackers.

Baby Reubens

40 slices of party rye
2 pkgs. of shredded swiss cheese
1 10 oz. can sauerkraut, rinsed
1/2 lb. sliced corn beef
dijon mustard

1. Place bread on baking sheet. Broil for 2 minutes.

2. Arrange corn beef, mustard and sauerkraut on bread.

3. Broil for 5 minutes.

4. Serve.

Bacon and Chunky Clam Dip

10 slices well done bacon, crumbled
2 6 oz. cans minced clams
½ cup sour cream
8 oz. softened cream cheese
2 scallions, finely chopped
½ tsp. Worcestershire sauce
1 tsp. lemon juice
1 tsp. white horseradish sauce
½ cup finely chopped red pepper

1. Blend all ingredients in medium mixing bowl and refrigerate for 2 hours before serving.

2. Can be served with torn pieces of italian bread or chips.

Bacon Wrapped Scallops

24 large real scallops, cleaned
12 slices of bacon, cut in half
Salt
Pepper
Garlic Powder

Preparation:

1. Preheat broiler.

2. Combine 1/2 tsp. salt and 1/2 tsp. pepper with 1 tsp. of garlic powder.

3. Wrap scallop with bacon strip and secure with toothpick.

4. Sprinkle salt mixture on scallop.

5. Place in broiler for 5–8 minutes.

6. Serve.

Baked Artichoke Pastry

1 can biscuits
1 can artichoke hearts, chopped
1 tsp. cayenne pepper
1 cup cheddar cheese, shredded
1 green onion, chopped
1 tsp. garlic powder
1/4 tsp. oregano

1. Preheat oven as indicated on biscuit can.

2. Combine all ingredients in bowl.

3. Separate biscuits with fingers to make a pocket and stuff with mixture.

4. Bake for 10 minutes and serve.

Baked Artichoke Dip

1 Rye or Pumpernickel Bread, Round
1 lb. shredded cheddar cheese
7 green onions, chopped
1 can artichoke hearts, chopped
1 16 oz. sour cream
1 8 oz. whipped cream cheese
1 tbsp. prepared chopped garlic, 4 garlic cloves, chopped

1. Preheat oven to 350.

2. Cut medium size hole on top of bread. Remove inside of bread to hollow it out.

3. In small saute pan cook onions and garlic in 1 tbsp. butter.

4. In medium bowl combine all ingredients and blend well. Add in the onions and garlic mixture and blend well.

5. Scoop into bread mixture.

6. Place top of bread back on.

7. Cover bread completely in aluminum foil and bake for 60 minutes.

8. Serve with the pulled out bread or other breads or crackers.

Baked Clams

48 littleneck clams
1½ cups bread crumbs
4 cloves garlic, minced
4 tbsp. roasted peppers, minced
4 tbsp. olive oil
1 tbsp. oregano

1. First clean clams. Pry them open with a butter knife (it is safer than steak knife). Cut out the clam and reserve in bowl. Save one side of the clam shell for serving. We will need 48 halves.

2. In small bowl combine bread crumbs, garlic, peppers, oil and oregano. Mix well. Now with the clams, I prefer to chop up all the clams into little pieces (my preference). If you choose to chop them up mix the chopped clams with other ingredients and spoon mixture into clams shells. If you choose not to, take whole clams and place back in shell and spoon mixture over clam.

3. Place clams on large cookie sheet and bake for about 10 minutes. If you like you can garnish with parmesan cheese and lemon.

4. Please make sure before placing clam back into shell that you clean them well.

Barbecue Cocktail Meatballs

2 lb. ground beef
1 onion, finely chopped
1/2 cup milk
1/2 bread crumbs
2 eggs
1/2 tsp. salt
1 cup barbecue sauce
1/2 cup water
1/2 cup apricot jam

Preparation:

1. Combine beef, onion, milk, bread crumbs, eggs and salt. Mix well and make into small balls. Bake in oven for 45 minutes.

2. In large sauce pan add in barbecue sauce, water and jam. Add in meatballs and let simmer on low for 10 minutes.

3. Serve with toothpicks.

Barbecue Mini Meatballs

2 lbs. chopmeat
2 cups barbecue sauce (any brand)
2 eggs
1 cup italian bread crumbs
2 tsp. garlic powder
1 tsp. onion powder
1 medium onion, finely chopped
1 cup beer
1/2 cup milk
1/2 cup oil

1. Blend all ingredients together except oil.

2. Make meatballs about the width of a quarter.

3. You can either fry them on top of the stove or bake them in the oven with the remaining barbecue sauce.

4. If you fry them heat them for 5-10 minutes in the oven in the remaining barbecue sauce.

Bell Pepper Dip

1 large green bell pepper
1 large red bell pepper
1 large yellow bell pepper
1 cup sour cream
1 cup mayonnaise
2 tsp. parmesan cheese
1 tsp. paprika
1/2 tsp. parsley
1 tbsp oil

1. Cut and remove the seeds from the peppers. Chop the peppers into small pieces and saute in heated oil for 5-10 minutes. Remove from heat and place in food processor or blender.

2. Add in all ingredients and blend until smooth.

3. Refrigerate for at least 30 minutes.

Cancun Stuffed Mushrooms

2 lbs. mushroom, cleaned and stemed
2 tsp. garlic powder
1/2 cup soy sauce
1 lb. spicy sausage
3 green onions, diced
1/2 tsp. salt
1/2 tsp. pepper
1 tsp. oil

1. Cut sausage into tiny pieces and fry in oil until browned.

2. In bowl add sausage, garlic powder, soy sauce, onin, salt and pepper. Blend well.

3. Spoon mixture into mushrooms.

4. Bake for 20-25 minutes at 350.

Cannelloni Brushetta

2 13 oz. cans cannelloni beans, drained and rinsed
1 tsp. olive oil
1 tsp. salt
1 4 oz. jar sweet red pimentos
1 large french bread, cut into 1/2 inch slices

1. In food processor or blender combine beans, olive oil, salt and pimentos. Blend until smooth.

2. Preheat oven to broil. Place bread on cookie sheet and broil for 1 minute.

3. Spread bean mixture onto bread and broil for 3-5 minutes. Watching carefully not to burn.

4. Serve on nice dish.

Caper and Garlic Vegetable Dip

2 tbsp. capers
3 tbsp. parsley
5 garlic cloves, chopped
½ cup chives
1 egg
1 tsp. dijon mustard
1 cup sour cream
¼ cup vegetable oil
½ cup olive oil
½ tsp. pepper
¼ tsp. salt
2 tsp. lemon juice
Food Processor or Blender

1. In food processor or blender combine capers, garlic, chives and parsley. Process until chopped fine.

2. Add in the egg, mustard, salt, pepper and lemon juice. For about 5 seconds.

3. Put the processor on slow blend and and in the olive and vegetable oil. When done it should have the consistency of mayonnaise.

4. Add in the sour cream and blend well again. Taste to see if it needs more salt, pepper or lemon juice.

5. Chill overnight and serve with fresh vegetables.

Cheese Ball Spread

1 8oz. whipped cream cheese
1/2 lb. grated cheddar cheese
1/2 lb. meunster cheese
10 pimento olives, finely chopped
pinch of salt
1/4 tsp. cayenne pepper
2 tbsp. mayonaise
1/2 tsp. garlic powder
2 tsp. worcestershire sauce

Preparation:

1. In medium bowl add all ingredients aand blend well. You might want to use your bare hands. Mold into ball or even log.

2. You can roll in chopped nuts or even paprika.

3. Refrigerate 2 hours and serve with crackers.

Cheese Buns

12 hot dog buns
1 lb. cheddar cheese, grated
1 stick of butter

Preparation:

1. In large bowl combine butter and grated cheese.

2. Open buns and spread mixture inside.

3. Place on large cookie sheet and broil for 3−5 minutes.

4. Remove from oven and slice bun into 6 pieces and serve.

Chicken Tenders with Dipping Sauce

3 lbs. chicken tenders
3 eggs
1 cup water
2 cups bread crumbs
1 16 oz. sour cream
1 18 oz. barbecue sauce, any flavor

1. Heat oven to 375 degrees.

2. Combine eggs and water. Dip chicken tenders into egg mixture and cover with bread crumbs.

3. Place on baking dish and bake for 50 minutes.

4. In small bowl combine barbecue sauce and sour cream. Chill for 30 minutes before serving.

5. Arrange on platter and serve or place 3-4 pieces on each plate and top with heaping spoonful of sour cream mixture and serve as appetizer first course.

Chinese Chicken Wings

3 dozen chicken wings
3 cups water
1 cup soy sauce
1 tbsp. sugar
1/2 cup oil
1/2 cup oyster sauce
1/2 cup white wine

1. Mix all ingredients together except for chicken wings.

2. Preheat oven to 350F.

3. Place chicken wings in baking dish and pour over mixture.

4. Bake for 30 minutes. 5. Serve with plenty of napkins.

Corn Salsa

2 cans drained corn
3 tbsp. lime juise
4 tbsp. olive oil
1 large tomatoe, diced and seeded
1 15 oz. can black beans rinsed and drained
1 red onions, finely chopped
3 tbsp. parsley
2 tbsp. red wine vinegar

Preparation:

1. In bowl combine all ingredients and refrigerate for 2 hours.

2. Add salt and pepper to taste.

3. Serve with large tortilla chips.

Crab Cakes

1 lb. crabmeat
1/2 cup oil
1 tbsp. oil
5 shallots, minced
1 cup whipping cream
2 eggs
3 cups italian bread crumbs
1/2 white wine
2 tsp. garlic powder
4 scallions, chopped
1/4 cup horseradish sauce
1 cup parsley

1. In skillet heat 1 tbsp. oil and cook shallots and scallions. Cook until tender. Add in wine,
   whipping cream and horseradish sauce.

2. Let simmer for 5 minutes and let cool.

3. In large bowl combine this mixture with crabmeat, eggs, breadcrumbs and parsley.   Make
   into either 8 hamburger like patties or 32 small balls.

4. Heat 1/2 oil until hot and saute the crab cakes or balls in oil. Cook until all sides are golden brown.

5. You might want to top with a tsp. of horseradish on each cake or in the center of the 8.

Crabmeat Stuffed Mushrooms

24 mushrooms, cleaned
1 8 oz. whipped cream cheese
1 can (6 oz.) crabmeat
1 small onion, minced
1/2 tsp. horseradish
2 tbs.. bread crumbs
1 tsp. salt
1 tsp. worcestershire sauce
1 tbs.. milk

Preparation:

1. Combine all ingredients except mushrooms.

2. Preheat oven to 350 degrees.

3. Fill mushrooms with crabmeat mixture.

4. In large baking dish coat with 2 tbs.. of butter and bake mushrooms for 10 minutes.

Crab Meat Appetizer

4 lbs. cooked lump crab meat
3 cups mayonnaise, can be light
4 tbs. dijon mustard
1 red bell pepper, chopped
1 green bell pepper, chopped
1 cup chopped scallions
3 egg yolks
3 tbs. Worcestershire Sauce
2 tsp. tobasco sauce
½ tsp. salt
½ tsp. pepper
1 tsp. paprika

1. Heat oven to 375°.

2. In large bowl combine all ingredients, mixing well.

3. In medium casserole dish coat side with butter and bread crumbs. (You would use the same technique if you were coating a cake pan with butter than dusting with flour).

4. Add mixed ingredients to casserole dish and bake for 20−25 minutes. If the top has not browned at the end, turn on broiler for 1 minute.

5. Let cool for 15 minutes. Serve with crackers or little pieces of torn french bread.

Crabmeat Balls

2 7 oz. cans crabmeat
1 tsp. parsley
12 slices of bacon
1 cup seasoned bread crumbs
3 tbs.. cooking sherry
1 tbs.. lemon juice
1 tsp. onion powder
1 tsp. mustard
pinch salt
1 tsp. pepper

Preparation:

1. Lay bacon on papertowels and cover with papertowels. Place in microwave and cook for 10 minutes on high. Cook until totally brown and crispy. Remove and let cool. When cooled, place between papertowels again and crush with hands until you make all crumbs.

Crab Stuffed Mushrooms

24 mushrooms
1 can crab meat
1 egg, beaten with 2 tsp. milk
2 tsp. bread crumbs
1 small onion, finely chopped
1 cup parmesan cheese
1 tsp. garlic powder
1 tsp. onion powder
1/2 tsp. salt
2 tsp. parsley

1. Preheat oven to 300 degrees.

2. Clean mushrooms.

3. Combine remaining ingredients and stuff into mushrooms.

4. Bake for 20 minutes.

5. Serve.

Cream Cheese and Caviar Dip

1 12 oz. container whipped cream cheese
1 cup sour cream
1 small jar black caviar

Preparation:

1. Mix all ingredients well and refrigerate for 1 hour.

2. Serve as dip with crackers.

Cucumber Dip

2 large cucumbers
2 8 oz. pkgs. cream cheese
½ cup white vinegar
2 tsp. salt
½ tsp. garlic salt
3/4 cup mayonnaise

1. Peel cucumber skin off and then grate into medium slices.

2. Mix cucumber in vinegar and salt overnight.

3. In small mixing bowl add cream cheese, mayonnaise and garlic. Mix well.

4. Squeeze excess liquid from cucumber and mix cucumbers with cream cheese mixture and stir well.

5. Serve this with vegetables or tortilla chips.

Curried Yogurt Dip

1 cup plain yogurt
1 tsp. hot sauce
pinch of black pepper
2 tsp. curry powder
1 tsp. lemon juice
1 tsp. sugar

1. Combine all ingredients and blend well.

2. Refrigerate 20 minutes before serving.

3. Serve with vegetables.

Deep Fried Pork Meatballs

1½ lbs. pork chop meat
1½ cups red bell pepper
1½ cup finely chopped onion
½ cup chopped garlic
1 tsp. garlic powder
1 tsp. salt
1 tsp. cayenne pepper
½ tsp. black pepper
1 stick butter
1 cup flour
vegetable oil
2 eggs
1 cup water
2 cups bread crumbs

Preparation:

1. First in medium fry pan heat butter until melted and add in flour. Mix well and heat until creamy a dark beige color. Add in onions and red pepper and heat for 10 minutes and remove from heat.

2. In large fry cook pork in about ¼ cup oil. Brown well and remove from heat.

3. In medium bowl combine meat and onion and pepper mixture with hands, be sure to make sure both are cool first. Let sit in the refrigerator for about 1-2 hours.

4. When chilled, roll into small balls. Mix eggs with water and leave in bowl for dipping pork balls. Place bread crumbs in separate bowl.

5. First, dip pork balls into egg mixture then coat well with bread crumbs. Do this step to all of the meat before starting to cook.

6. In large sauce pot, cover bottom of pot with 2 inches of oil and heat on medium to high. The oil has to high enough to submerse the pork ball. Place as many pork balls in very hot oil and cook for 5-8 minutes, sometimes longer. You will be able to tell.

7. In small bowl combine mustard and mayonnaise. To serve place heaping teaspoon in middle of dish and place pork balls around it. Serve as a first course or appetizer.

Deviled Eggs Lisa

12 hard boiled eggs
3 tbsp. dijon mustard
2 scallions, finely chopped
6 tbsp. mayonnaise
2 tsp. parsley
2 tsp. lemon juice
1½ tsp. curry powder
½ tsp. dry mustard
¼ tsp. salt
½ tsp. pepper
Paprika

1. Cut eggs in half lengthwise and take out yolks and reserve in bowl.

2. Mash yolks and mix in all ingredients except Paprika.

3. Spoon mixture into eggs and sprinkle with Paprika.

4. Serve 3 each for first course or can be used as an appetizer.

Easy Herb Spread

1 16 oz. whipped cream cheese
1 tsp. garlic powder
2 scallions, minced
1 tsp. mustard
1/2 cup parsley
1/2 cup basil

1. Combine all ingredients well.

2. Place in pretty bowl and refrigerate for at least 1 hour before serving.

3. Serve with crackers.

English Muffin Crab Cakes

8 whole english muffins
2 6 oz. cans crabmeat
2 tbsp. mayonaise
1 tsp. garlic powder
1 tsp. onion powder
1/2 tsp. salt
1/2 tsp. pepper
1 small onion, diced
1 16 oz. pkg. shredded meunster cheese

1. Split english muffins and bake on cookie sheet for 10-15 minutes or until turning slightly brown.

2. In medium bowl combine remaining ingredients. Blend well.

3. Remove english muffins from oven and place spoonfuls of crabmeat mixture on top of muffins.

4. Bake for 15 minutes or until cheese is bubbly.

5. If you have extra mixture, place in small baking dish and bake for 10 minutes and serve with crackers.

Five Cheese Baked Ziti

Sauce:

2 large cans crushed tomatoes
2 small cans tomato sauce
2 small cans tomato paste
1 medium onion, chopped
4 garlic cloves, chopped
1 tsp. salt
1 tbsp. garlic powder
1 tbsp. onion powder
2 tsp. chili powder
1 tsp. pepper

Ziti:

2 lbs. ziti
2 15 oz. pkgs. of ricotta cheese, skim or whole
2 cups shredded swiss cheese
2 cups parmesan cheese
2 cups shredded provolone
2 cups crumbled bleu cheese

1. Make sauce first. Combine all ingredients and simmer for 1 hour or until ready to use.

2. In large bowl combine all the remaining ingredients and mix well. Add in half the sauce and mix well.

3. When ziti is cooked drain very well and add in to sauce and cheese mixture. Mix well.

4. In 1 or 2 baking dishes pour in ziti mixture and you may want to add some sauce to the top and garnish with sauce and parsley.

5. Bake at 350° for 45 minutes. Let set in oven for 15 more minutes and serve.

6. Serve with salad and bread.

Fried Meat Ravioli

1 lb. frozen meat ravioli
2 cups seasoned bread crumbs
1 cup oil
2 eggs, beaten
3 tbsp. water
1 jar premade alfredo sauce

1. Combine eggs and water. Dip ravioli into egg mixture and then into bread crumbs.

2. Heat oil in large skillet and fry ravioli until golden brown.

3. Place on papertowel to remove excess grease.

4. Heat alfredo sauce on stove or in microwave. Place in bowl to serve.

5. Arrange ravioli on dish around alfredo sauce.

Fried Mozzarella with Roasted Pepper Sauce

2 jars roasted peppers
¼ cup olive oil
¼ cup water
¼ cup red wine vinegar
1 tsp. garlic powder
1 tbsp. cayenne pepper
1 tsp. salt
½ tsp. pepper
3 16 oz. pkgs. of mozzarella
2 cups bread crumbs
1½ cups vegetable oil
2 eggs, beaten with ¼ cup of water

1. Slice mozzarella into slices (approximately 15 per pkg.) Dip mozzarella in egg mixture and then into bread crumbs just like you would to chicken cutlets. Do all pieces of cheese before starting to fry, it makes it easier.

2. Heat 1½ cups of oil in large fry pan. Place cheese cutlets in fry pan, do not over crowd. Let brown on both sides watching carefully not to melt cheese all over the place.

3. When done set aside on serving platter.

4. In medium sauce pan heat olive oil, roasted peppers, garlic powder, salt, pepper, water, red wine vinegar and cayenne pepper. When warmed pour mixture into blender and pulse until creamy.

5. The sauce can be poured into small ramekins so all your guests have their own sauce and are not dipping into the same dish.

Fried Tomatoes

2 eggs
6 large red tomatoes, cut into 4 slices each
2 cups bread crumbs
2 cups olive oil
1 strip of bacon (optional)
3 cups mayonnaise
½ cup mustard, any kind
1 tsp. salt
1 small onion, diced
1 tsp. pepper
1 tsp. cayenne pepper
¼ cup parsley
¼ cup thyme

1. Heat oil in large fry pan.

2. Make egg wash with the eggs, add a little water.

3. Dip tomatoes in egg and then in bread crumbs.

4. Place in fry pan and fry until golden brown on both sides.

5. Set aside on paper towel to remove excess oil.

6. To make sauce, mix together mayonnaise, mustard, onion, salt, pepper, cayenne. parsley and thyme. Mix well.

7. On salad plate place three tomatoes in an arrangement and place a large tablespoon of mayonnaise in the middle.

Garlic and Blue Cheese Bread

1 large loaf french bread, slice down the middle
1 8 oz. chunky blue cheese dressing
1 8 oz. whipped butter, softened
2 tbsp. garlic powder
1 cup parmesan cheese

1. Preheat oven to 350.

2. In small bowl combine blue cheese dressing, garlic, and parmesan cheese.

3. Spread each loaf of bread with butter.

4. Spread on blue cheese and parmesan mixture. 5. Bake for 15−20 minutes.

Garlic Clam Dip

1 8 oz. whipped cream cheese
2 tsp. lemon juice
2 tsp. worcestershire sauce
1/2tsp. salt
1/2garlic powder
1 tsp. pepper
1 7 oz. can minced clams, with juice

Preparation:

1. Combine all ingredients except clam juice. Mix well. If you want a thinner spread add some clam juice.

2. Serve with crackers or vegetables.

Sauteed Goat Cheese Cakes

1 cup leeks, diced
1 lb. goat cheese
1 cup flour
1 cup bread crumbs
2 eggs, beaten with water
½ cup garlic, minced
1 tsp. salt
½ tsp. pepper
1 tsp. cayenne pepper

1. In large fry pan saute leek until soft. Empty into medium bowl. Add in goat cheese, at room temperature, garlic, salt, pepper and cayenne pepper. Mix well with hands. Make shapes the size of a flattened egg.

2. Dip goat cheese shape into flour, egg and bread crumbs. Fry on medium heat until golden brown.

3. Serve with salad.

Hot Stuffed Mushrooms

24 mushrooms, cleaned
2 eggs, beaten
2 cups crabmeat
1 tsp. onion powder
2 tbsp. parmesan cheese
2 tsp. parsley
1 tbsp. hot sauce
1 tsp. cayenne pepper
2 tbsp. bread crumbs
1 tsp. salt

1. Preheat oven to 325.

2. Combine all ingredients except mushrooms.

3. Spoon in mixture to mushrooms and bake for 20 minutes.

Hot Wings

5 lbs. chicken wings
1 lb. butter
1 8 oz. can tomato sauce
4 tsp. cayenne pepper
2 tsp. garlic powder
1 tsp. black pepper
3 tsp. tobasco sauce
2 cups pancake syrup
1 tsp. onion powder

1. Bake chicken wings at 400 degrees until thoroughly cooked, depending on size.

2. Mix all other ingredients and set aside.

3. Remove wings from oven and place in sauce mixture.

4. Serve with a lot of napkins.

Italian Bread Boat Dip

2 Large loaves italian bread
1 cup onions, chopped
1½ cups crab dip
1 cup cheddar cheese
1 cup mayonnaise

1. Hollow out one loaf of bread using the pulled out pieces as bite size dipping pieces. Tear up the whole second loaf and use as dipping pieces.

2. Mix together in baking dish onions, crab, cheddar and mayonnaise. Bake for about 10 minutes or until hot.

3. Pour mixture into hollowed out loaf of bread and serve.

Jumbo Garlic Shrimp

48 jumbo shrimps, cleaned and deveined
4 tbsp. cayenne pepper
6 tbsp. garlic powder
2 cups olive oil

1. In large bowl combine oil, cayenne pepper and garlic powder. Blend well and add in the shrimp. Coat the shrimp well.

2. Heat skillet and saute shrimp half at a time.

3. When done place in large bowl and use toothpicks or serve 6 on a plate as first course.

Little Franks with Orange Dipping Sauce

1 pkg. cocktail franks
2 cup orange juice
1/2 cup pancake syrup

Preparation:

1. In medium sauce pan heat orange juice and pancake syrup. Bring to simmer and add in cocktail franks.

2. Let simmer for 10 minutes.

3. Serve in pretty bowl with toothpicks.

Marinated Mushrooms

1 lb. fresh mushrooms
1 tsp. chives
1 cup red wine vinegar
1/2 cup olive oil
1 tsp. tarragon
pinch of salt
1/2 cup water
1 tsp. garlic powder

1. Clean and dry mushrooms.

2. Mix all ingredients together.

3. Let marinate in refrigerator for 8-12 hours.

4. Serve.

Mashed Potato Stuffed Mushrooms

24 mushrooms, cleaned and stemed
4 large baking potatoes
1 8 oz. whipped cream cheese
1 cup finely chopped shrimp
1/2 stick of butter
1 tsp. salt

1. Bake potatoes in microwave for 12 minutes. Let cool and scoop out the potato.

2. In medium bowl combine potato, cream cheese, shrimp, butter and salt Blend well.

3. Spoon mixture into mushrooms and bake for 10−15 minutes at 325.

Mexican Dip

1 lb. ground beef
1 tbsp. chilli powder
1 tsp. cayenne pepper
1 onion, diced
1 small chile or jalapeno, diced
1 16 oz. whipped cream cheese
1 bag shredded cheddar cheese

1. In saute pan brown meat and onion. Add in chilli powder, cayenne pepper and jalapeno.

2. In bowl combine meat, cream cheese and cheddar cheese.

3. Place in baking dish and bake for 15 minutes.

Mixed Cheese Spread

1 8 oz. pkg. of whipped cream cheese
4 oz. bleu cheese
1 cheddar cheese, grated
2 tbsp. worcestershire sauce
1 cup cooked, cut up meat (ham or sausage)
1/2 cup butter
1 onion, finely chopped

Preparation:

1. In large bowl combine all cheese with mixer.

2. Add in all ingredients and refrigerate for 8 hours and serve.

3. Serve with small breads or crackers.

Mozzarella Sticks with Spicy Sauce

40 mozzarella sticks
1 16 oz. premade plain spaghetti sauce
1 medium onion, diced
1 tbsp. red pepper flakes
1 tsp. cayenne pepper
1 tsp. salt
1 tsp. pepper
dash of hot sauce
1 tsp. olive oil

1. Bake mozzarella sticks as indicated on pkg.

2. In medium sauce pan heat onions in oil. Add in remaining ingredients.

3. Heat sauce for 30 minutes or length of cooking time for mozzarella sticks.

Mushroom and Nut Pate

2 lbs. mushrooms, chopped
1 cup nuts, any kind
2 tbsp. vegetable oil
1/2 tsp. pepper
1 tbsp. tarragon
2 tbsp. lemon juice
1 tsp. paprika
1 tsp. salt
1 cup plain yogurt
1 small onion, finely chopped
1 tbsp. garlic powder
Parsley for garnish, not necessary

Preparation:

1. In large skillet heat in oil onion and garlic. Cook until tunring golden brown. Add in garlic powder, mushrooms. Stir in tarragon, lemon juice, salt, pepper and paprika.

2. Remove from heat and let stand for 5 minutes. Place in blender and blend for 3 minutes. Add in nuts (almonds) and chop them. Blend for 2 more minutes.

3. Refrigerate for 8 hours and serve with crackers.

Mushroom & Sun Dried Tomato Spread

½ lb. fresh mushrooms
½ lb. portabella mushrooms
½ cup chopped sun dried tomatoes
¼ cup green onions, chopped
3 garlic cloves
2 loaves french bread, cut into diagonal slices
1 tbsp. olive oil

1. In food processor or blender puree all ingredients.

2. Toast bread in oven until lightly browned. Place bread on serving dish or bowl.

3. Place mushroom mixture into bowl. Spread mixture into bread and serve or have each person do their own.

Mushroom Bread

1 small loaf white bread
1/2 lb. mushrooms, finely chopped
2 tsp. lemon juice
1 cup heavy cream
1/2 tsp. salt
1/2 tsp. garlic powder
3 tbsp. flour
1/4 cup butter
1 scallion, finely chopped

Preparation:

1. Sauter mushrooms in butter. Add in lemon juice, heavy cream, salt, garlic powder, flour and scallions.

2. Cook until cramy and thick.

3. Preheat oven to 425.

4. Remove mushroom mixture from stove.

5. Dip bread into mixture on both side. Place on cookie sheet and bake on each side for 5–8 minutes.

Onion Rings with Dipping Sauce

2 large bags of onion rings
1 16 oz. whipped cream cheese
1 16 oz. sour cream
1 16 oz. salsa

1. Bake onion rings as indicated on bag.

2. In medium bowl combine all ingredients and blend well.

3. Refrigerate for at least 30 minutes before serving.

Pancake Syrup Chicken Wings

6 lbs. chicken wings
1 cup pancake syrup
3 tsp. garlic powder
1 cup soy sauce

1. Season wings with garlic powder.

2. Bake for 30 minutes at 325.

3. In small bowl combine syrup and soy sauce.

4. Pour over chicken wings and bake for 10 more minutes.

Peanut Chili Dip

1/2 cup creamy peanut butter
1 tbsp. chili powder
2 tbsp. honey
3 tbsp. water
2 tbsp. soy sauce
1 tsp. garlic powder

Preparation:

1. In bowl combine all ingredients until blended well. If mixture seems to thick add more water.

2. Serve with carrots, broccoli, green and red peppers.

Pesto Crescents

1 8 oz. can crescent rolls
2 tbsp. parmesan cheese
1 egg yolk
6 tsp., sun dried tomatoes in oil
3 tbps. pesto sauce (use envelope)
1 tbsp. water

Preparation:

1. Open crescent roll can.

2. In bowl combine parmesan cheese, sundried tomates and pesto sauce. Mix well.

3. Open each individual crescent and place 1 tbsp. of mixture into center. Fold over like a triangle. Press edges down firmly with fork.

4. In small bowl mix together egg and water and with finger paint the egg mixture over the crescent.

5. Bake for 10−15 minutes or until golden brown.

Pierogies with Sour Cream

32 pierogies, any kind
2 16 oz. sour creams
2 tbsp. paprika
1 small onion
3 tbsp. butter
1 tsp. olive oil

1. In small saute pan heat butter and oil.

2. Lay pierogies on large baking dish and pour over oil and butter mixture. Bake for 35 minutes, or until they are turning golden brown.

3. You might want to toss once or twice while cooking.

4. Five minutes before complete sprinkle over the paprika.

5. Serve on large plate and place sour cream in bowl in center.

Pork Tenderloin with Roasted Garlic Mayonnaise

1 12 oz. Pork Tenderlointlets
5 tbsp. olive oil
½ tsp. salt
½ tsp. pepper
¼ cup romano or parmesan cheese
1 cup parsley
1 Whole Garlic, Medium Head
½ cup mayonnaise

1. Preheat oven to 325°. In long mixing dish or pan combine parsley, salt, pepper and cheese. Coat pork tenderloin with oil on all sides and cover with the parsley mixture.

2. Place in baking dish with 4 tbsp. of oil and bake uncovered for about 45 minutes to an hour. Also, take the first layer of skin off the garlic bulb and cut off the pointed top. Place in small baking dish with 2 tsp. of olive oil and bake for 45 minutes.

3. After 45 minutes let garlic cool and squeeze out the garlic like toothpaste. With the fork tines, press the garlic down. Mix with the mayonnaise well.

4. Remove pork from oven and let cool for 10 minutes. Cut into slices and serve two to each plate with a teaspoon of garlic mayonnaise on the side or on top of them. Garnish with some parsley.

Quick Stuffed Celery

1 bunch of celery, cleaned
1 8 oz. whipped cream cheese
2 tbsp. sour cream
1 small can black olives, chopped
1 tsp. paprika

1. Combine cream cheese, sour cream, olives and paprika.

2. Fill celery stalk and serve.

Raisin Spread

1 cup raisins
1 8oz. whipped cream cheese
1 tsp. cinnamon

Preparation:

1. Mix together all ingredients and refrigerate for 1 hour.

2. Serve on bagels or toast.

Red Bell Pepper Pancakes

3/4 cup red bell pepper, diced
2/3 cup flour
1 tbsp. melted butter
2 large eggs, separated
¼ cup cornmeal
½ tsp. hot red pepper flakes
3 tbsp. coriander
1 pint sour cream

1. In large bowl mix together all ingredients except sour cream and egg whites. Add 1 tsp. salt and ¼ tsp. pepper.

2. In small bowl beat egg white until fluffy. Fold into flour mixture.

3. Heat large fry pan with some melted butter. Spoon in balls of the mixture into fry pan. Do not over crowd. Flatten the balls into small pancakes, about 1–2 inches in diameter. Cook each pancake 1 minute on each side or until golden brown.

4. These pancakes can be used as appetizers or as first course. For 8 guests, place 5 pancakes on each plate with a large tablespoonful of sour cream. Garnish with parsley.

Salmon Dip

1 can salmon
1 8 oz. whipped cream cheese
1 cup onions, finely chopped

Preparation:

1. Mix all ingredients and refrigerate for 2–4 hours before serving.

Salsa with Shrimp

64 jumbo shrimps
4 16 oz. jars of salsa
½ tsp. salt
½ tsp. pepper

1. In large sauce pan heat the salsa until very hot. Stirring constantly.

2. Add in all the shrimp at once and cook thoroughly for 5 minutes.

3. Place in large serving bowl.

4. You can serve this with white rice. Very fast and delicious dish for the salsa lover.

Sausage Dip

3 lbs. skinny italian sausage, frozen
1 cup mayonaise
1 cup sour cream
1/2 tsp. pepper
pinch of salt
1/2 tsp. paprika
1 tsp. cayenne pepper

1. Cut sausage into 1 inch pieces. Either fry in frying pan or cook in oven.

2. Mix mayonnaise, sour cream, pepper, salt, paprika and cayenne pepper. Blend well and refrigerate.

3. Use sauce to dip in sausage. Serve with toothpicks.

Sauteed Mushrooms

2 lbs. mushrooms, sliced in half
2 garlic cloves, chopped
1 tsp. hot red pepper flakes
1 stick butter
½ Sherry
½ cup Teriyaki Sauce
2 tbsp. parsley

1. In large fry pan cook garlic and pepper flakes in butter on low heat. Add in mushrooms, teriyaki sauce and sherry and cook over medium heat until mushrooms are tender.

2. Remove mushrooms and bring liquid to boil until thickened like syrup.

3. Add in parsley and salt and pepper to taste. Return mushrooms to heat and serve.

4. Can serve with any meat.

Sauteed Mushrooms in Biscuits

2 Pkgs. Refrigerated Biscuits, raw
½ lb. shitake mushrooms
½ lb. fresh mushrooms
½ lb. portabella mushrooms
2 cups scallions, chopped finely
1 cups balsamic vinegar
4 cloves garlic, minced
½ tsp. salt
½ tsp. pepper
1 lemon
½ stick of butter

1. In large saute pan heat all mushrooms in butter with scallions, garlic, salt and pepper. When mushrooms cooked and tender place in blender or food processor and pulse until finely chopped.

2. Place back in saute pan. Add in balsamic vinegar and the juice of lemon. heat for 5 minutes.

3. Grease cookie sheet if necessary. Cut biscuits in half. To be safe when doing this, place biscuit on counter and cut from right to left or maybe you can even peel them apart.

4. When the biscuits are separated, place a tbsp. of mushroom mixture in the middle and place the top of the biscuit back on top. To make sure the insides don't fall out press the whole perimeter of the biscuit.

5.   Bake for 8 minutes on 325°.

Sesame Chicken

24 chicken tenders
1 cup sesame seeds
4 tbsp. dijon mustard
2 tsp. onion powder
2 cups mayo
1 cup honey

1. Grease baking sheet. Preheat oven to 450.

2. Combine dijon mustard, onion powder, mayo and honey. Dip chicken tenders into this mixture and then into sesame seeds.

3. Place chicken tenders on baking sheet and bake for 20-25 minutes.

Spinach and Bacon Dip

1 cup mayonaise
1 cup sour cream
1 pkg. frozen chopped spinach
8 slices of bacon
1 tsp. garlic powder
1/2 tsp. red pepper flakes

1. If you can, cook the bacon in microwave until very crispy. Let cool and break into tiny pieces.

2. Place spinach in strainer – squeeze to remove all excess water.

3. In medium bowl add all ingredients well.

4. Refrigerate at least 1 hour.

5. Serve with fruit, vegetables, chips or breads.

Spinach Dip

1 pkg. chopped spinach, cooked and drained
1 pkg. vegetable soup mix
1 8 oz. sour cream
1 cup mayonaise

Preparation:

1. Mix all ingredients well and refrigerate for 8 hours.

2. Serve with crackers.

Sweet Potato Appetizers

2 40 oz. cans sweet potatoes
1 stick of butter
2 cups bread crumbs
2 cups pancake syrup
1 tsp. salt
1/2 tsp. pepper

1. In bowl mash potatoes. Add in butter, pancake syrup, salt and pepper.

2. Make into golf ball size balls. Roll in bread crumbs.

3. Preheat oven to 350 and bake for 30 minutes.

4. Serve as an appetizer or with a ham or turkey dinner.

Tomato and Basil Bruschetta

1 loaf of french bread, makes 24 pieces
4 garlic cloves
¼ cup basil
2 lbs. seeded tomatoes, diced
6 tbsp. olive oil

1. Heat oven to 375°.

2. Cut bread into 4 inch long pieces. Brush pieces of bread with olive oil. Toast in oven for about 10 minutes or until golden brown.

3. After toasting, rub garlic on the toast. Mix remaining olive oil and tomatoes and basil in bowl. Add salt & pepper to taste. Top each piece of toast with about tsp. of mixture.

4. Place on dish and serve.

Tomato Potato Skins

8 large baking potatoes
2 tomatoes, finely chopped
1 cup shredded mozzarella
1 cup shredded cheddar
4 green onions, chopped
1 tsp. olive oil
2 tsp. cayenne pepper
1 tsp. salt
1 tsp. onion powder
1 tsp. chili powder
1 16 oz. sour cream

1. Microwave potatoes for 3 minutes each, which should be 24 minutes.

2. Cut potatoes in half lengthwise. Scoop out potato middles.

3. In medium bowl combine potato middles with tomatoes, mozzarella, cheddar, onions, olive oil, cayenne, salt, onion powder and chili powder. Blend well.

4. Spoon mixture back into potato shells and bake for 10−15 minutes.

CPSIA information can be obtained
at www.ICGtesting.com
Printed in the USA
LVHW021356280122
709444LV00011B/629